MW01178474

Measurement

From the Read-Aloud Anthology

ONE INCH TALL

by Shel Silverstein

Access Prior Knowledge
This poem will help you review
- Addition and subtraction facts through 12
- Concept of length

ISBN-13: 978-0-618-59091-9
ISBN-10: 0-618-59091-9
ISBN-13: 978-0-618-67182-3
ISBN-10: 0-618-67182-X

456789-WC-14 13 12 11 10 09 08 07   Printed in the U.S.A.

ONE INCH TALL

If you were only one inch tall, you'd ride a worm to school.

The teardrop of a crying ant would be your swimming pool.

A crumb of cake would be a feast

And last you seven days at least,

A flea would be a frightening beast

If you were one inch tall.

If you were only one inch tall, you'd walk beneath the door,

And it would take about a month to get down to the store.

A bit of fluff would be your bed,

You'd swing upon a spider's thread,

And wear a thimble on your head

If you were one inch tall.

You'd surf across the kitchen sink upon a stick of gum.

You couldn't hug your mama, you'd just have to hug her thumb.

You'd run from people's feet in fright,

To move a pen would take all night,

(This poem took fourteen years to write—

'Cause I'm just one inch tall).

Name_____

Use the number line.
Solve.

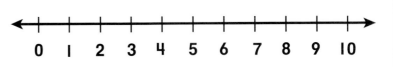

0 1 2 3 4 5 6 7 8 9 10

Draw or write to explain.

1. One worm is 6 inches long.
   Another worm is 4 inches long.
   They stretch along the number
   line end to end. How long are
   they altogether?

   _____ inches

2. A blue bird sees 4 worms.
   A red bird sees 6 worms.
   How many more worms does
   the red bird see?

   _____ more worms

3. A baby worm is 1 inch
   long. It grows 6 inches.
   How long is it now?

   _____ inches

4. Some worms are 2 inches
   long. A group of them stretch
   along a 10-inch twig.
   How many worms are there?

   Skip count
   by 2s.

   _____ worms

5. **Talk About It** What would you do if you were
   one inch tall?

Dear Family,

My class is starting Unit 7. I will be learning about length and weight. I will also be learning about capacity and temperature. These two pages show what I will learn and have activities for us to do together.

From, _____

Vocabulary

These are some words I will use in this unit.

pound	A customary unit of weight
kilogram	A metric unit of mass

cup, pint, quart, liter   Units to measure capacity

thermometer   An instrument that measures how hot or cold something is

Some other words I will use are **measure**, **inches**, **centimeters**, and **weight**.

Vocabulary Activity

Let's work together to complete these sentences.

1. _____ and _____ are used to measure how heavy an object is.

2. Capacity can be measured using _____ ,

   _____ , _____ , and _____ .

3. This instrument tells us how hot or cold something is. _____

Turn the page for more.

How To measure objects with a ruler

In this unit I will be measuring objects. I will be using an inch ruler to measure length and height.

Measure

About how many inches long is the pencil?

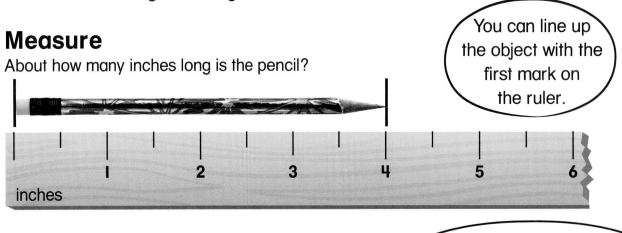

> You can line up the object with the first mark on the ruler.

_____ inches

About how many inches long is the pencil?

> You can also line up the object with any inch mark on the ruler.

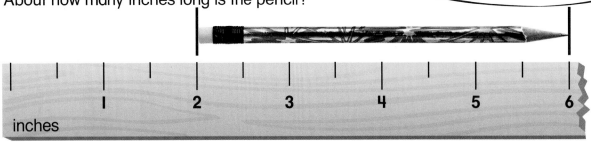

Count the spaces between the inch marks at both ends of the object.

_____ inches

◆ Literature

These books link to the math in this unit. We can look for them at the library.

Inch by Inch
by Leo Lionni
(Bt Bound, 1999)

Measuring Penny
by Loreen Leedy

Lulu's Lemonade
by Barbara deRubertis

> Let's read together!

Education Place

We can visit *Education Place* at

eduplace.com/maf

for the Math Lingo game, *e*•Glossary, and more games and activities to do together.

Name_____

Centimeters

You can also measure length with **centimeters**.
Estimate the length.

Estimate: about ___10___ centimeters

Objective
Estimate and measure an object in centimeters using a ruler.

Vocabulary
centimeters

⊢—⊣
I centimeter

Use a centimeter ruler to measure the length.

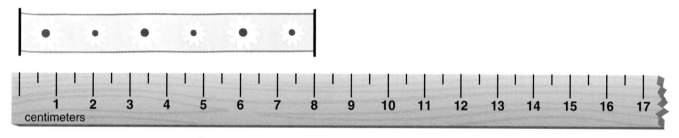

Measure: about ___8___ centimeters

Guided Practice

First estimate.
Then use a centimeter ruler to measure.

1.

Estimate: about _____ centimeters Measure: about _____ centimeters

---

2.

Estimate: about _____ centimeters

Measure: about _____ centimeters

Explain Your Thinking Name three objects that are
shorter than 10 centimeters.

Remember to use the end marks to help you measure.

First estimate.

Then use a centimeter ruler to measure.

1.

Estimate: about _____ centimeters | Measure: about __17__ centimeters

2.

Estimate: about _____ centimeters | Measure: about _____ centimeters

3.

Estimate: about _____ centimeters | Measure: about _____ centimeters

4.

Estimate: about _____ centimeters

Measure: about _____ centimeters

Reading Math ▶ Vocabulary

5. Color the shortest feather [crayon].

6. Color the longest feather [crayon].

7. Circle the feather that is about **6** centimeters long.

At Home Ask your child to find objects at home that are longer than 10 centimeters. Then measure the objects.

 Go on

Activity

Name_____

Measure Up

2 to 4 Players

What You Need: cubes, centimeter ruler, pencil, paper clip, and items on the spinner

How to Play

1. Take turns.
   Spin the spinner.

2. Find that object.

3. Use a centimeter ruler to measure the object.

4. Take cubes to match the number of centimeters.

5. Group the cubes by 10s.
   Play until one player has 50 cubes.

Other Ways to Play

A. Use an inch ruler.
   Play until one player has 20 cubes.

B. Two players spin and measure. The player with the longest object scores 1 point. Play until one player has 5 points.

Find the object.

Is the object longer or shorter than your hand?

Circle.

1.
longer

shorter

2.
longer

shorter

Complete the chart.

3.

Find the object.	Measure with .
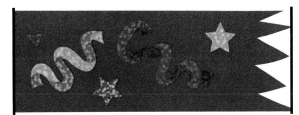	 about _____

First estimate.

Then use an inch ruler to measure.

4.

Estimate: about _____ inches

Measure: about _____ inches

First estimate.

Then use a centimeter ruler to measure.

5.

Estimate: about _____ centimeters

Measure: about _____ centimeters

Facts Practice, see page 679

Name_____

Activity: Compare Weight

 Audio Tutor 2/16 Listen and Understand

You can compare the **weight** of objects.
Use a balance scale to find which is
heavier and which is **lighter.**

Objective
Compare and order the weight of objects using nonstandard units.

Vocabulary
weight
heavier
lighter

Step 1

Find two objects.
Estimate.
Which feels heavier?
Which feels lighter?

The book feels much heavier than the pencil.

Step 2

Put the objects
on a balance scale.
Compare the weight.

The side with the book is lower. The book is heavier.

Work Together

Find the objects.
Circle the heavier object.

1.

2.

3.

4.
 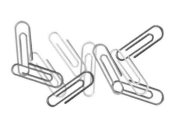

5. **Talk About It** Name three objects you could put in a balance scale to use as units to measure weight.

Choose a unit to measure the weight.

Make both sides of the balance scale equal.

Find the object.	Record the measure.	Circle the unit.
6.	about _____	🖇 ⬜
7.	about _____	🖇 ⬜

On Your Own

Number the objects in order from lightest to heaviest.

The object that is the lightest is 1.

1.

_____   _____   _____

Circle the object that weighs about the same as two boxes.

2.    

3. **Write About It** How do you know that two objects weigh about the same?

_____

_____

At Home Choose two kitchen objects. Ask your child which is heavier and which is lighter.

Name_____

Activity: Pounds

Objective
Compare and order the weight of objects.

Vocabulary
pounds

Hands-On

You can measure weight in **pounds.**

Step 1

Find the object.
Find a 1-pound weight.

less than 1 pound

Step 2

Weigh the objects on a balance scale.

about 1 pound

more than 1 pound

> The juice is the heaviest object.
> The soup is the lightest object.

Work Together

Compare the weight to 1 pound.
Circle.

Think
The side that is lower is more than 1 pound.

1.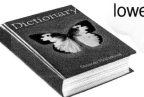

less than

about the same

more than

2.

less than

about the same

more than

3.

less than

about the same

more than

4. **Talk About It** Order the objects in Exercises 1–3 from lightest to heaviest.

Remember to think about objects you measured on the balance scale.

Circle.

Use  if the object weighs more than 1 pound.

Use  if the object weighs less than 1 pound.

1.

---

2. Pedro has these coins.
   He buys a mask for 50¢.
   How much money does
   he have left?

   _____¢

3. **Write About It** What coins could Pedro have left?

   _____

At Home Have your child find three food items that weigh about 1 pound.

Name_____

Activity: Kilograms

 Audio Tutor 2 / 18 Listen and Understand

Objective
Compare objects to
a kilogram.
Vocabulary
kilograms

You can measure how heavy an
object is in **kilograms.**

Step 1

Find the object.
Find an object that
is 1 kilogram.

less than 1 kilogram

Step 2

Put the objects on
a balance scale.

about 1 kilogram

more than 1 kilogram

Think
The side that is higher is
the side that is less than.

Work Together

Compare the object to 1 kilogram.
Circle.

1.

less than

about the same

more than

2.

less than

about the same

more than

3.

less than

about the same

more than

4.

less than

about the same

more than

5. **Talk About It** Would you measure the length of a pencil
in kilograms or centimeters? Why?

Remember to think about objects you measured on the balance scale.

Circle.

Use ▭▭▭▶ if the object is more than 1 kilogram.

Use ▭▭▭▶ if the object is less than 1 kilogram.

1.

Write 9, 90, or 900 under each picture.

2.

about

about

about

_____ kilograms   _____ kilograms   _____ kilograms

3. **Write About It** How heavy do you think you are

in kilograms?_____

At Home Help your child find three food items labeled in kilograms.
Then compare them to find which is the heaviest and which is the lightest.

Name_____

Use Logical Reasoning

Objective
Use logical reasoning to solve word problems.

Problem Solving

You can use clues to solve a problem.

Noelle wants a jump rope with handles.
She wants one shorter than the purple rope.
Which jump rope should she choose?

THINK

Noelle wants a jump rope with handles.

Noelle wants a jump rope shorter than the purple one.

Which jump rope should Noelle choose?

DECIDE

The green jump rope does not have handles.

Cross out the green jump rope.

She does not want the purple jump rope.

Cross out the purple jump rope.

Not the green. Not the purple. Noelle should choose the yellow jump rope.

Circle the yellow jump rope.

The yellow jump rope makes sense. It has handles. It is shorter than the purple jump rope.

Solve.

Circle the object that matches the clues.

1. It has squares on it. It is smaller than the orange ball.

   Think
   Cross out the ball with the dots.
   Find the one that is smaller
   than the orange ball.

2. It is longer than the red bat.
   It is made out of metal.

   Think
   Cross out the red bat.
   Find the one that is metal.

Practice

3. It is blue. It is taller than the pink chalk.

4. It has handles.
   It is not the longest jump rope.

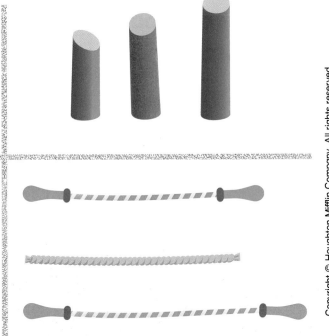

At Home Ask your child to explain how he or she used the clues to solve the problems.

Name_____

Now Try This **Using a Ruler**

Use an inch ruler to measure.

1.

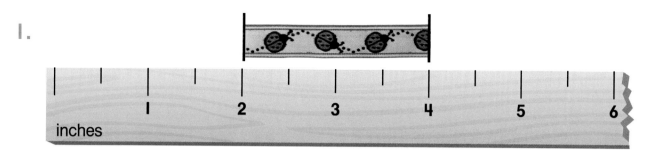

Measure: about __*2*__ inches

2.

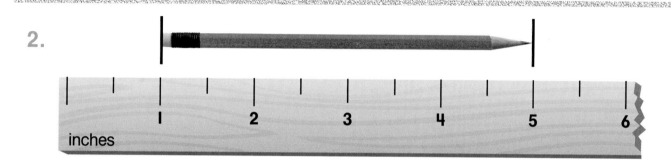

Measure: about _____ inches

Use a centimeter ruler to measure the length.

3.

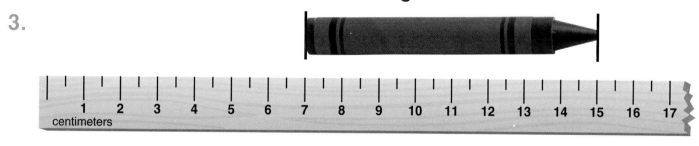

Measure: about _____ centimeters

4.

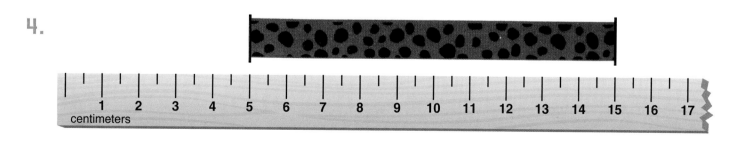

Measure: about _____ centimeters

Social Studies Connection
Growing Luca

Luca lives in Florida. His parents measure him. He is **48** inches tall.

Luca's aunt from Rome, Italy comes to visit. His aunt measures him. Luca is **122** centimeters tall.

Did Luca grow? What happened?

_____

_____

Key Topic Review — Time

Read the clock. Write the time.

1.

_____ o'clock

2.

half past _____

3.

_____ o'clock

4.

_____ : _____

5.

_____ : _____

6.

_____ : _____

Extra Practice at **eduplace.com/map**

Chapter Review/Test

Vocabulary

Match the word to the correct statement.

1. **heavier**   a unit to measure length

2. **pound**   an object that weighs more

3. **centimeter**   a unit to measure weight

4. **height**   a measurement of how tall something is

Concepts and Skills

Find the object.
Is the object longer or shorter than your hand?
Circle.

5.   longer

            shorter

6.   longer

            shorter

Choose a unit to measure the length.

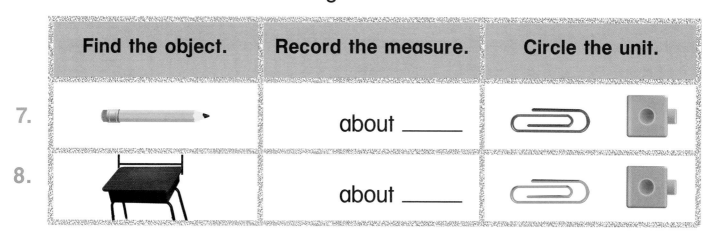

Find the object.	Record the measure.	Circle the unit.
7.	about _____	
8.	about _____	

First estimate.
Then use an inch ruler to measure.

9.

Estimate: about _____ inches

Measure: about _____ inches

First estimate.

Then use a centimeter ruler to measure.

10.

Estimate: about _____ centimeters | Measure: about _____ centimeters

Circle the heavier object.

11.

12.

Circle the objects that weigh more than I pound.

13.

Circle the objects that are more than I kilogram.

14.

Problem Solving

Solve.

Circle the bat that matches the clues.

15. It is made out of wood.
It is not the longest bat.

Capacity and Temperature

INVESTIGATION

Find the object that can hold the most water.

PEOPLE USING MATH
Ben Franklin

Ben Franklin playing his armonica.

Benjamin Franklin was an important person in our country in the 1700s. He was also a famous inventor who enjoyed music. Franklin once saw musical glasses filled with water. Different tunes were played on them. He invented an instrument called the armonica. Sounds are created on the instrument by rubbing water on different shaped glasses.

You Can Make Your Own Musical Glasses

The amount of water and thickness of the glasses can change the tune. Songs like "Twinkle, Twinkle, Little Star," "The Itsy, Bitsy Spider," or "I'm a Little Tea Pot" can be played on the glasses.

Name_____

Activity: Compare and Order Capacity

Compare the containers.
Find the container that can hold more.

> **Objective**
> Compare and order the capacity of containers.

Use containers.
Fill one container.

Pour it into the other container.

The pail is not full. So, the pail can hold more.

Work Together

Circle the container that can hold more.

1.

Think
Pour from the glass into the jar.

2.

Circle the container that can hold less.

3.

4.

5. **Talk About It** Choose three containers from the exercises above. Put them in order from the greatest amount to the least amount they can hold.

On Your Own

Number the objects.
1 holds the least amount.
3 holds the greatest amount.

1.

   1   3   2

2.

   _____   _____   _____

3.

   _____   _____   _____

4.

   _____   _____   _____

5. **Talk About It** Name three other containers you could use as units to measure capacity.

6. Color the smallest box ▭▬▶ .
   Color the largest box ▭▬▶ .

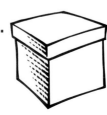  

At Home Show your child two different bowls. Ask which bowl can hold more. Pour water from one to the other to check the answer.

Name_____

Activity: Cups, Pints, and Quarts

 Audio Tutor 2/20 Listen and Understand

Objective
Compare the capacity of cups, pints, and quarts.
Vocabulary
cups pints quarts

Use **cups, pints,** and **quarts** to tell how much a container holds.

2 cups = 1 pint   2 pints = 1 quart

Step 1

Fill the smaller container.
Pour it into the larger container.

Step 2

Continue until the larger container is full.

 Work Together

Use cups, pints, and quarts.
Complete the table.

Count as you pour each container.

How many?	Number
1. cups in a pint	_____ cups
2. pints in a quart	_____ pints
3. cups in a quart	_____ cups

4. **Talk About It** How many cups of milk fill a 1-quart container? How do you know?

On Your Own

Use cups, pints, and quarts to compare.
Circle the one that holds more.

1.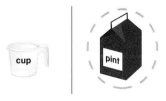

2.

3.

4.

Circle the ones that hold the same amount.

5.

6.

7. How many more cups does the vase hold than the mug?

_____ more cups

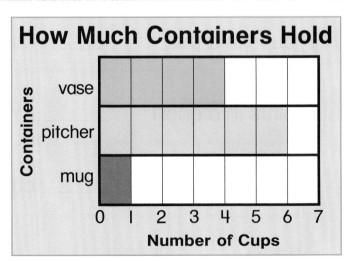

8. **Talk About It** Create a question you can answer by using the graph.

At Home Ask your child to find containers at home that can hold 1 cup, 1 pint, and 1 quart.

Name_____

Activity: Liters

 Audio Tutor 2/21 Listen and Understand

You can also use **liters** to tell how much a container can hold.

Hands-On

 Step 1

Fill a liter bottle.
Find the container.

The vase is not full. So, the vase can hold more than 1 liter.

 Step 2

Pour the liter bottle into the container.

less than 1 liter   1 liter   more than 1 liter

Work Together

Compare to 1 liter.
Circle.

Think
Does the liter bottle fill the vase?

1.
   less than
   about the same
   more than

2.
   less than
   about the same
   more than

3.
   less than
   about the same
   more than

4.
   less than
   about the same
   more than

5. **Talk About It** Would you use a liter container to fill a swimming pool? Why?

Remember to think about objects you measured with the liter bottle.

Circle.

Use ▭ if the object can hold more than 1 liter.

Use ▭ if the object can hold less than 1 liter.

1.

Circle the containers that can hold more than 1 liter.

2.

Remember this is 1 liter.

Go on

Number the objects.

1 holds the least amount.

3 holds the greatest amount.

3.

_____ 1 _____ 3 _____ 2

4.

_____ _____ _____

5.

_____ _____ _____

Underline the words that tell how much a container can hold.

Circle the words that tell how long an object is.

6. cup

7. liter

8. centimeter

9. quart

10. pint

11. inch

12. **Write About It** What other containers can hold more than **1** liter? _____

_____

Number the objects.

1 holds the least amount.

3 holds the greatest amount.

1.

_____   _____   _____

Circle which can hold the same amount.

2.  |  |

3. |  |

Circle the objects that can hold more than 1 liter.

4.

Circle the objects that can hold less than 1 liter.

5.

Facts Practice, see page 679

Temperature

You can use the words **hot** and **cold** to describe the **temperature.**

Use a **thermometer** to measure temperature.

Objective
Understand hot and cold.
Vocabulary
hot   cold
temperature
thermometer
degrees

The temperature is **90 degrees.**

The temperature is **30** degrees.

Guided Practice

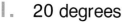

Circle **hot** or **cold** to tell about the temperature.

1. 20 degrees

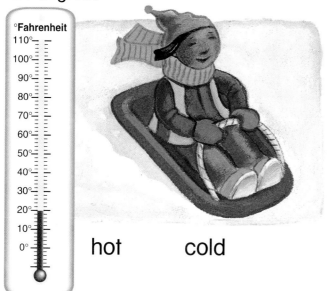

hot   cold

2. 85 degrees

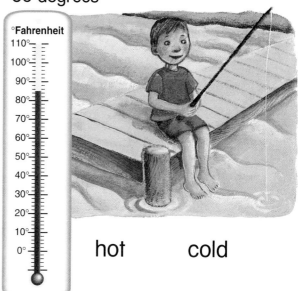

hot   cold

Explain Your Thinking Look at all the temperatures. Which is the hottest? Which is the coldest?

Circle **hot** or **cold** to tell about the temperature.

1. 10 degrees

hot   ⟨cold⟩

2. 80 degrees

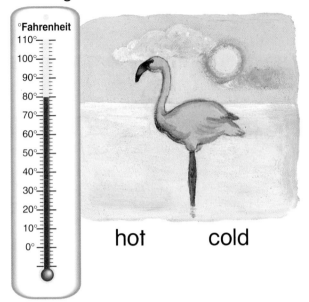

hot   cold

3. 100 degrees

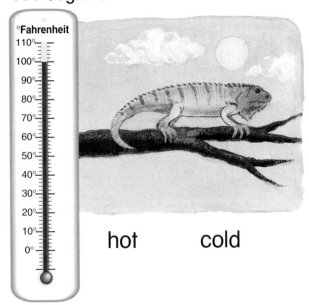

hot   cold

4. 25 degrees

hot   cold

Problem Solving ▶ Reasoning

Order the pictures 1, 2, and 3.
Write 1 for the coldest. Write 3 for the hottest.

5. 55 degrees   30 degrees    90 degrees

_____   _____   _____

534 five hundred thirty-four

At Home Ask your child to identify familiar foods as **hot** or **cold**.

Name_____

Reasonable Answers

Choose the answer that makes more sense.

Dawn makes a terrarium. She puts pebbles, soil, and plants into a bowl. She needs to find out if a tall plant will fit.

What should she use to measure the height of the plant?

Objective
Choose the more reasonable measuring tool to solve problems.

THINK

DECIDE

Dawn needs to measure the height of the plant.	She needs to choose a measuring tool.
A ruler measures length or height.	She needs to measure the height of the plant.
A balance scale measures how heavy something is.	She does not need to know how heavy the plant is.
Which tool should Dawn use?	The ruler. It measures height.

The ruler is the more reasonable answer. It makes more sense.

Circle the answer that makes more sense.

1. Jimmy wants to know how long the side of the fish tank is. What can he use to find out?

Think
Which measures how long something is?

2. Tyler wants to know how much water is in his fish tank. What can he use to find out?

Think
Which measures how much something holds?

3. Maia has a stone and a rock. What can she use to find out which is heavier?

4. Pete needs to know the temperature of the water in his fish tank. What can he use to measure?

At Home Ask your child to tell why the answers he or she chose are reasonable and why the others do not make sense.

Name_____

Now Try This **Compare Capacity**

1. Draw three bowls.

   Bowl A holds the most.
   Bowl B holds the least.

   _____   _____   _____
      A   B   C

2. Draw three cups.

   Cups D and E hold the same amount.
   Cup F holds more than E.

   _____   _____   _____
      D   E   F

3. Draw three bottles.

   Bottle G holds more than H.
   Bottle I holds more than G.

   _____   _____   _____
      G   H   I

4. **Talk About It** Look at Exercise 3. Which bottle did you draw first? How did it help you draw the other bottles?

Social Studies Connection
Johnnycakes

Native Americans grew corn and
made it into cornmeal. Johnnycakes
were made from cornmeal. They
are like pancakes and could
be taken on long trips, or journeys.

Pioneers called them "journey cakes"
or johnnycakes.

1 cup of cornmeal makes johnnycakes for 4 people.
How many cups of cornmeal do you need for 8 people?

_____ cups

WEEKLY WR READER eduplace.com/map

Money

Circle the coins that match the price.

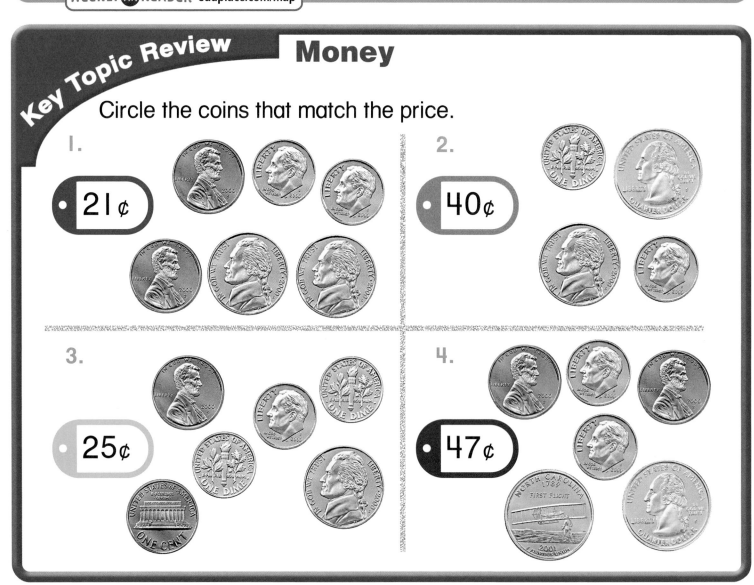

1. 21¢

2. 40¢

3. 25¢

4. 47¢

Extra Practice at **eduplace.com/map**

Name_____

 Chapter Review/Test

Vocabulary

Complete the sentence.

cups	liters	thermometer

1. There are 2 _____ in a pint.

2. A _____ tells you how hot or cold something is.

3. You can use _____ to tell how much a container holds.

Concepts and Skills

Circle the container that can hold more.

4.

5.

Number the objects.
1 holds the least amount.
3 holds the greatest amount.

6.

_____   _____   _____

Circle which holds more.

7.
  |

8.
  |

Chapter Review/Test

Circle which can hold the same amount.

9.

10.

Circle.

Use  if the object can hold more than 1 liter.
Use  if the object can hold less than 1 liter.

11.

Circle **hot** or **cold** to tell about the temperature.

12. 20 degrees

hot   cold

13. 80 degrees

hot   cold

14. 40 degrees

hot   cold

Problem Solving

Circle the answer that makes more sense.

15. Megan wants to know if she
needs to wear a jacket outside.
What should she use to find out?

540 five hundred forty

Name_____

Exploring Area

You can find the area of a plane shape
by using square units.

Use the square unit.
Estimate the area.
Find the area.

Think
I can put 1 square
unit in the corner to
help me estimate.

1.

Estimate: about _____ square units

Measure: about _____ square units

2.

Estimate: about _____ square units

Measure: about _____ square units

3.

Estimate: about _____ square units

Measure: about _____ square units

Education Place
See **eduplace.com/map**
for brain teasers.

Calculator
Fill It Up!

There are **2** pints in **I** quart.
How many pints are in **5** quarts?

Use a .

Find the number of pints in **5** quarts.

Press: **2** **+** **2** **=** [**4**]

> Each time you press **=** ,
> 2 more will be added.

Press: **=** **=** **=** [**10**]   _____ pints

Use a 🖩 .
Complete the table.

1.

Pints	I pint	2 pints	3 pints	4 pints
Cups	2 cups	____ cups	____ cups	____ cups

2.

Quarts	I quart	2 quarts	3 quarts	4 quarts
Pints	2 pints	____ pints	____ pints	____ pints

3.

Quarts	I quart	2 quarts	3 quarts	4 quarts
Cups	4 cups	____ cups	____ cups	____ cups

Explain Your Thinking Which is greater, **6** cups or
4 pints? Why?

Name_____  **Unit 7 Test**

Vocabulary

Match the word to the correct statement.

1. **inch**   a measure of how heavy an object is

2. **weight**   a unit to measure temperature

3. **degree**   a unit to measure length

4. **pound**   a unit to measure weight

Concepts and Skills

First estimate.

Then use an inch ruler to measure.

5.

Estimate: about _____ inches   Measure: about _____ inches

First estimate.

Then use a centimeter ruler to measure.

6.

Estimate: about _____ centimeters Measure: about _____ centimeters

Circle the heavier object.

7.    8.

Circle the objects that weigh more than 1 pound.

9.

✓ Unit 7 Test

Circle the objects that are more than **I** kilogram.

10.

Circle which holds more.

11. |

12.  |

Circle **hot** or **cold** to tell about the temperature.

13. 10 degrees

hot   cold

14. 90 degrees

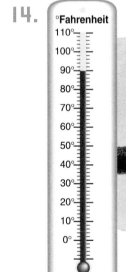

hot   cold

Problem Solving

Circle the answer that makes more sense.

15. Christos wants to measure milk to make a cake. Which tool should he use?

544 five hundred forty-four

Test-Taking Tips

• •

Make a drawing to help solve a problem.

Narrow the choices by quickly finding the ones that cannot be correct.

Multiple Choice

Fill in the ○ for the correct answer.

1. About how long is the feather?

1 inch	3 inches
○	○

6 inches	10 inches
○	○

2. Which of these weighs about 1 pound?

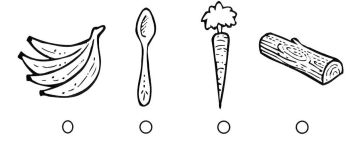

○   ○   ○   ○

3. What is the missing addend?

$$7 + \boxed{} = 12$$

2	3	4	5
○	○	○	○

4. What comes next in this pattern?

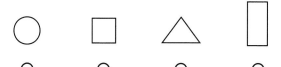

○   ○   ○   ○

Multiple Choice

Fill in the ○ for the correct answer.
NH means Not Here.

5. Which equals 1 quart?

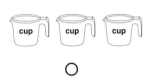
○

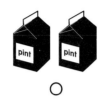
○

6. Which container holds more than 1 liter?

○   ○   ○

7. The temperature is 25 degrees. What should Dara wear when she goes outside?

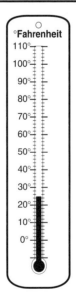

○   ○   ○   NH
                              ○

Open Response

Solve.

8. Anton needs 3 pints of milk in a recipe. He only has a 1-cup measure. How many cups of milk does he need?

_____ cups

9. The Garcia family makes 12 tacos. They eat 9. Then they make 2 more. How many tacos do they have now?

_____ tacos

10. How much is there in all?

_____ ¢

 Education Place
Look for Cumulative Test Prep at
eduplace.com/map for more practice.

546 five hundred forty-six

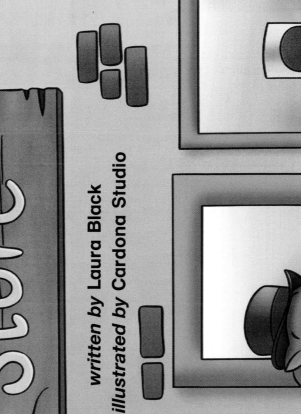

Squirrel's Store

written by Laura Black
illustrated by Cardona Studio

READING MATH

Shopping Time

Look back at the story to answer these questions.

▲ 1. Look at pages 2–3. Did Mrs. Pig buy more corn than Mr. Elephant bought peanuts?

■ 2. Look at page 4. If Squirrel only gives the birds one pack of seeds, how many seeds would they buy?

● 3. Look at page 6. How many more carrots does little rabbit need if he wants to buy 30 carrots?

☆ 4. Make up your own story about shopping at Squirrel's Store.

Answers
1. yes   2. 10   3. 8   4. Answers may vary.

Reading Strategies

▲ Noting Details   ● Cause and Effect
■ Infer   ☆ Summarize

8

Good day, Mr. Elephant.
What will you buy?
That's a lot of peanuts
For just one guy!

How many peanuts will Mr. Elephant buy?

It's been a very good day
At my little store.
Now it's time to get my things
And head out the door!

How many acorns will Squirrel take home?

2

7

Good day, Mrs. Pig.

What's in your cart?

Stocking up on corn,

That's pretty smart!

How many ears of corn will Mrs. Pig buy?

Good day, little rabbit.

What a tricky way to shop!

With so many carrots,

It must be hard to hop!

How many carrots will the little rabbit buy?

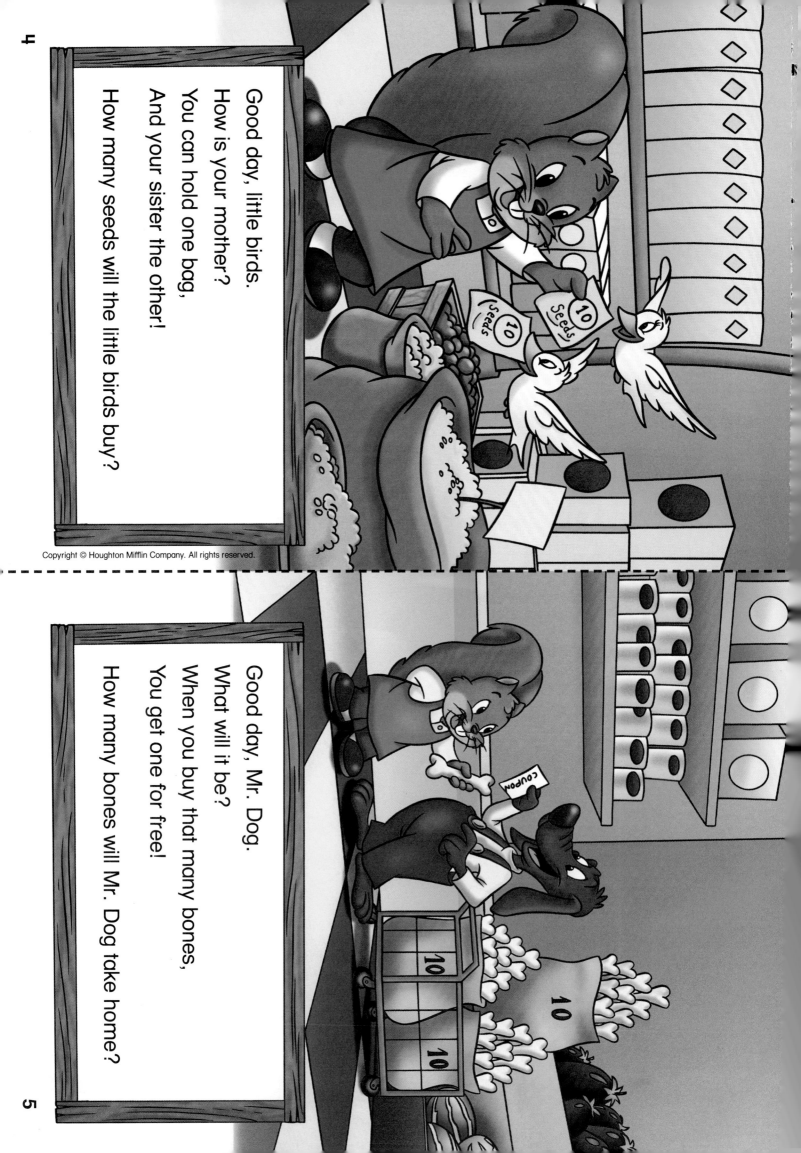

Good day, little birds.
How is your mother?
You can hold one bag,
And your sister the other!
How many seeds will the little birds buy?

4

Good day, Mr. Dog.
What will it be?
When you buy that many bones,
You get one for free!
How many bones will Mr. Dog take home?

5